SCHOLASTIC
NEWS
Nonfiction Readers

Octopuses

And Other Animals With Amazing Senses

by
Susan Labella

Children's Press®
A Division of Scholastic Inc.
New York Toronto London Auckland Sydney
Mexico City New Delhi Hong Kong
Danbury, Connecticut

These content vocabulary word builders
are for grades 1-2.

Consultant: William Fink
Professor of Ecology and Evolutionary Biology
University of Michigan
Ann Arbor, Michigan

Curriculum Specialist: Linda Bullock

Special thanks to Omaha's Henry Doorly Zoo

Photo Credits:

Photographs © 2005: Corbis Images: 23 top right (David A. Northcott), 20 top left (Jeffrey L. Rotman), 23 top left (Lawson Wood); Dave Welling: 4 bottom right, 15; Dembinsky Photo Assoc.: 5 top left, 13 (Dominique Braud), right cover inset (Skip Moody), left cover inset (Jim Roetzel); Dwight R. Kuhn Photography: 4 bottom left, 19, 23 bottom right; NHPA/Matt Bain: 18; Peter Arnold Inc.: 5 top right, 11, 20 top right, 21 top left (Fred Bavendam), 23 bottom left (Steven Kazlowski), center cover inset (Klein), 1, 5 bottom left, 10 (Jeffrey L. Rotman); Photo Researchers, NY: 4 top, 8, 9 (Eiichi Kurasawa), 5 bottom right, 17 (Andy Rouse); Seapics.com: 20 bottom right (Bob Cranston), 2, 7 (Reinhard Dirscherl), 21 center right (Jeff Rotman); Getty Images/Stuart Westmorland/The Image Bank: 21 bottom left; Visuals Unlimited: back cover (Ken Lucas), cover background (Mark Norman).

Book Design: Simonsays Design!

Library of Congress Cataloging-in-Publication Data

Labella, Susan, 1948-
  Octopuses and other animals with amazing senses / by Susan Labella.
  p. cm. — (Scholastic news nonfiction readers)
  Includes bibliographical references and index.
  ISBN 0-516-24928-2 (lib. bdg.)
    1. Animal defenses—Juvenile literature. 2. Octopuses—Juvenile litera-
    ture. I. Title. II. Series.
  QL759.L33 2005
  573.8—dc22
                                                            2005003097

1 2 3 4 5 6 7 8 9 10 R 14 13 12 11 10 09 08 07 06 05

CONTENTS

WORD HUNT

Look for these words as you read. They will be in **bold**.

ink
(ingk)

owl
(oul)

skunk
(skuhngk)

monarch
(**mahn**-ark)

octopus
(**ok**-tuh-puhss)

suction cup
suhk-shuhn kup)

wolf
(wulf)

Senses! Senses!

Animals have senses just like people do.

Smelling, tasting, touching, seeing, and hearing are senses.

Animals use their senses in many ways.

Let's find out more about how animals use their senses!

This is a day octopus.
It is swimming.

An **octopus** uses its sense of sight to stay safe.

If it sees an enemy, it will shoot black **ink** into the water.

Ink

Look! This octopus is shooting ink!

An octopus uses its sense of taste and touch, too.

An octopus has eight arms.

There are **suction cups** on each arm.

The cups help the octopus taste and touch its food.

suction cup

This is a Pacific giant octopus.
It is the largest octopus in the world!

Monarch butterflies use their sense of taste, too.

They taste leaves with their feet to find a place to lay their eggs.

The butterflies want to make sure the leaves are the right kind of food.

When the eggs hatch, the babies will eat the leaves.

A **skunk** uses its sense of sight to stay safe.

If a skunk sees an enemy, watch out!

The skunk lifts its tail to spray a smelly juice.

The juice hurts the enemy's eyes.

Run! This skunk is getting ready to spray!

15

A **wolf** has an amazing sense of smell.

It can smell other animals that are near.

This helps the wolf stay safe.

This helps it to find food, too.

Did you know that dogs and wolves belong to the same family?

17

An **owl** uses its sense of hearing to hear enemies.

An owl has ear openings on the sides of its head.

These openings help owls hear better than all other birds!

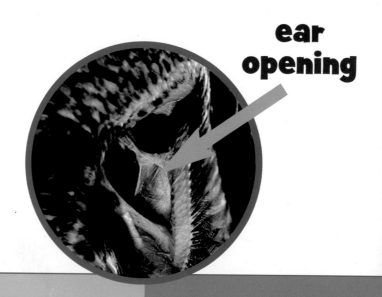

ear opening

an ear
opening

AN OCTOPUS SEES AN ENEMY!

1 Many octopuses live deep in the ocean. They use their sense of sight to see enemies.

2 This octopus sees a diver. The diver is too close. The octopus is scared.

Now, the diver can't see. The octopus can swim away.

4

The octopus shoots out black ink.

3

YOUR NEW WORDS

ink (ingk) a dark liquid that an octopus shoots out so its enemies can't see it

monarch (**mahn**-ark) a black and yellow butterfly

octopus (**ok**-tuh-puhss) a sea animal with eight arms

owl (oul) a bird with large eyes and a hooked beak

skunk (skuhngk) a black and white animal that sprays a smelly juice when it is afraid

suction cup (**suhk**-shuhn kup) round cups on the arms of an octopus

wolf (wulf) an animal in the dog family

THESE ANIMALS HAVE AMAZING SENSES, TOO!

catfish

chameleon

seal

spider

INDEX

FIND OUT MORE

Book:

What Do You Do When Something Wants To Eat You?
by Steve Jenkins, Houghton Mifflin, 2001

Website:

Amazing Animal Senses
http://faculty.washington.edu/chudler/amaze.html

MEET THE AUTHOR:

Susan Labella is a writer of books, articles, and magazines for kids. She is the author of other books in the *Animal Survivors* series for *Scholastic News Nonfiction Readers*. She lives in rural Connecticut where she sees skunks, owls, and butterflies in her backyard.